HAPPY EASTER, MOUSE!

ISBN 978-0-545-33213-2

12 11 10 9 8 7 6 5 4 3 2 11 12 13 14 15 16/0

Printed in the U.S.A. 40

First Scholastic printing, April 2011

HAPPY EASTER, MOUSE!

Laura Numeroff
Felicia Bond

SCHOLASTIC INC.
New York Toronto London Auckland
Sydney Mexico City New Delhi Hong Kong

The night before Easter,
Mouse decorates some eggs.

When he wakes up on Easter morning, he finds a **yellow** egg under his covers.

Who put these **red** eggs on the counter?

Mouse spies a few **blue** eggs under the rocking chair . . .

. . . and four **orange** eggs
on the sofa.

Who balanced all these **purple** eggs on the table?

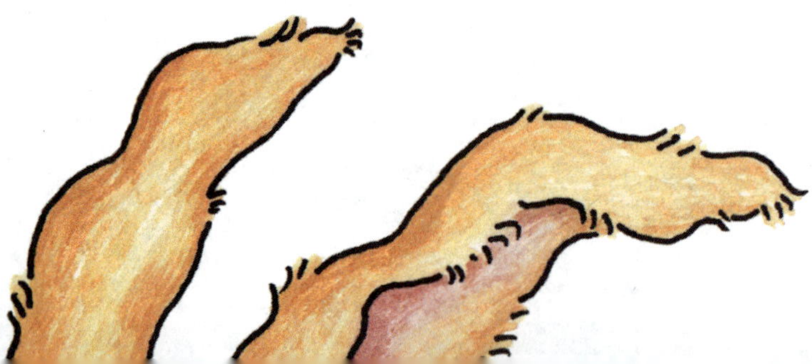

Mouse loves the **green** eggs
he finds on the desk.

He looks around. Who's hiding all these eggs?

It's Bunny!

Happy Easter,
Mouse!